## Pizza

## Triangle

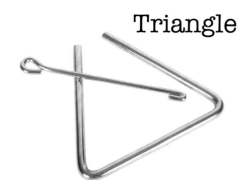

## Napkin

## Pool balls

Computer

Door

Cards

Brick

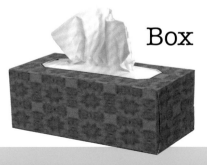

Box

Clock

Plate

Dart board

Lollipop

Orange

Picture frame

Note pad

Blocks

Pillow

Dice

# A diamond is a rotated square

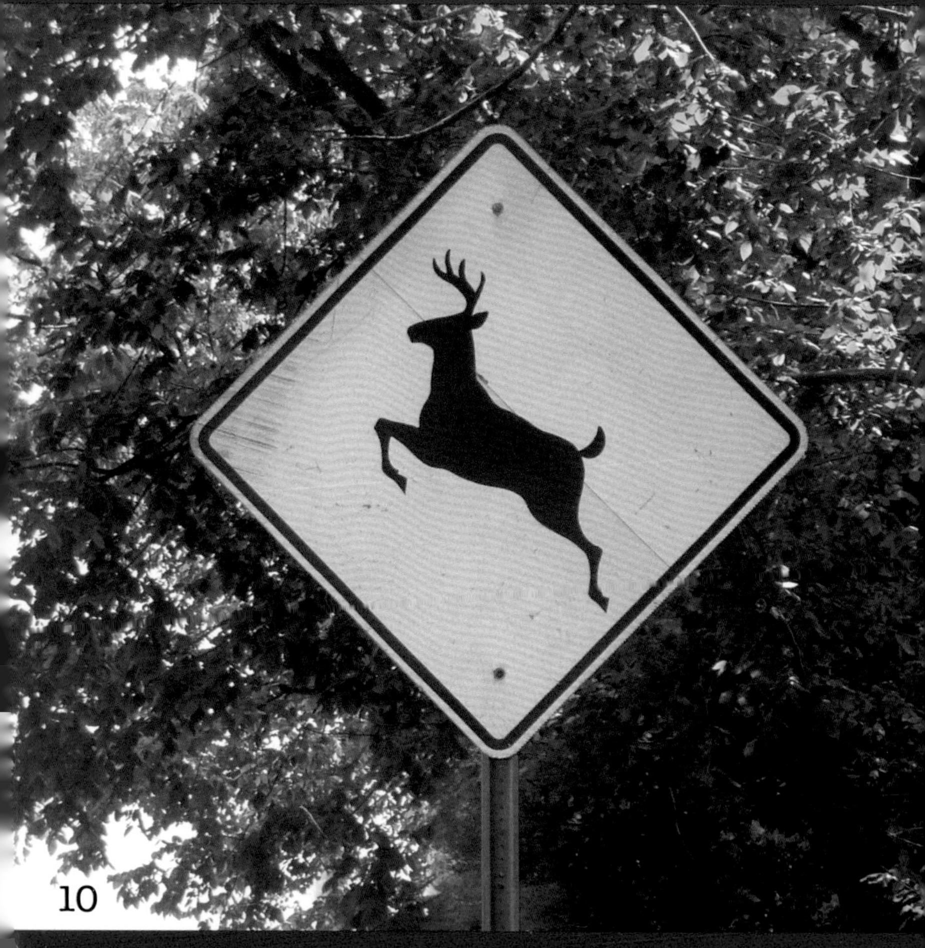

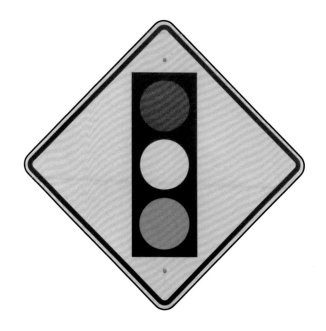

This is a yellow diamond,
a black rectangle
and three circles!

11

# Pentagons have 5 sides and hexagons have 6 sides

A soccer ball is made of pentagons and hexagons

School crossing

Nuts and bo

13

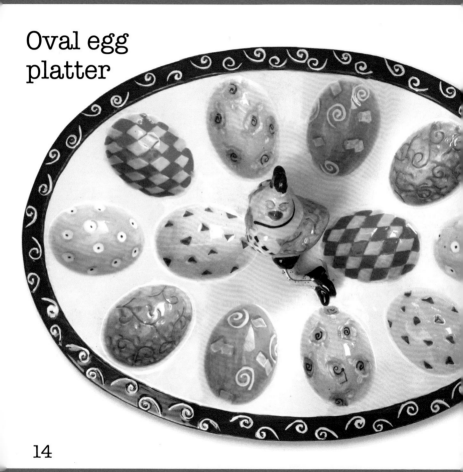

Oval egg
platter

14

Crescent

Heart

Stars

SHERIFF

15

The single most important way to help your children succeed in school is to read to them every single day.

Even before children can speak, books can help them learn sounds, shapes, colors, and the names of things

4614 Prospect Ave., Suite 328
Cleveland, Ohio 44103

(216) 881-0083 • NoodleSoup.com
Reprinted 04/21 • Product #9866

By Cydney Weingart

ISBN 978-0-9885075-

8 53738 00528